Poetry for All Seasons

Kaytlyn Hanner

BookLeaf
Publishing

India | USA | UK

Presentation by *BookLeaf Publishing*

Web: www.bookleafpub.com

E-mail: info@bookleafpub.com

ISBN : 9789357447720

First edition 2021

DEDICATION

To anyone who finds something they're looking
for within these pages

ACKNOWLEDGEMENT

I would like to thank my friends for encouraging me to reach for my dreams. My mom for reading my works and giving constructive criticism. Above all I'd like to thank my husband for always having faith in me even when I had a hard time having faith in myself.

The Seasons

He stepped quietly, softly through his
surroundings.
Most times, you wouldn't detect his presence
until it became overbearing.
He crept through quietly then seemed to take up
space all at once.
His quiet presence urged a contented sleep for
those around him.
He calmed the air and the trees; nudging animals
and plants alike into the long slumber.
He knew his calming presence would allow
Earth to rest.
Many saw him as death, but it was never death
he was dealing, it was peace.
He sought growth for his home and Autumn
knew without rest there would never be
progress.

On his heels his brother often rushed.
Winter would try to emerge before his time.
Anxious to deal the blows his brother Autumn
was hesitant to deal.
He would put out the lights.
He was power and fury and a beautiful
destruction followed in his wake.

He would often blanket entire provinces without
warning.
He would bring with him darkness and the brink
of death.
Where Autumn would be quiet and soothing,
Winter would rage!
He was loud and domineering, demanding
attention with only his presence.

He sister trekked slowly on his heels.
She was known to dawdle and take her time.
She brought life and warmth back to the
provinces Winter ravaged.
She was often timid, allowing Winter to ruin her
progress periodically.
He hated to give up his reign, even when it was
her turn.
She was gentle to wake Earth in the aftermath of
Winter's reign.
Spring was warm and gentle.
She was warmth and light.
She encouraged those that Autumn put to rest to
awaken reinvigorated with life.
Renewed and refreshed.

Then in marched Summer.
Summer was loud and Summer was boisterous.
Summer was fire and light.
She was heat and passion.

Summer came with urgency behind Spring.
She was a constant party.
She would push everyone and everything past
every limit they thought they might possess.
Summer rejoiced in frivolity.
Summer sought adventure and Summer begged
for spontaneity.
Then she would see her brother start his
approach and would slowly become calm as her
often quieted her loud with his soft.
Eventually Autumn's presence would nudge a
yawn from her.
She would yawn and yield as she began to
slumber with the Earth.

Autumn stepped quietly.

Life sometimes

Sometimes life is hard.
Sometimes life is easy.
Sometimes life is confusing.
Sometimes life makes you cry.
Sometimes life makes you laugh.
Life is...
wild,
calm,
exciting,
free,
life sometimes makes you question yourself.
life sometimes is a whirlwind.
life is hard to understand
and life is hard... just hard.
Things you like and things you hate,
they get mixed up in things you ain't.
You get lost in things you aren't.
and you get mixed up in expectations.
It's hard to think,
and say,
and be,
everything...

life sometimes...
is everything you need and more.

Life sometimes...
is this and that,
that you didn't expect,
when you weren't sure that it would ever be
more than,
life sometimes.

Geraldine

Seasons come and seasons pass,
nothing ever seems to last,
people part and come together,
old relationships seems to weather,
nothing ever stays brand new,
nothing can replace what's true.

Time goes on...
Now I wish the clock would stop,
I'm feeling selfish,
I want you to stay,
even for just one more day.

I need to tell you what I never did,
I love you...
Now I don't want you to go,
even though I know I'll see you again,
I still don't want to see the end.

Since this is it,
I'll say goodbye,
I'll keep your memories by my side,
and when I need to see you face,
I'll find a place,
I'll take them out and stop a while,

I'll remember you always with a smile,
I'll remember all you did,
when I was just a kid,

A kid who's wonder you always shared,
A kid for whom you really cared,
I'll miss you always and for evermore,
I know you're not suffering anymore.

You're an Angel now.
You'll be born again.

I Remember (for Gran)

I remember your laugh.
I remember your smile.
I remember the smell of your perfume.
I remember you.

I remember your eyes.
I remember your face.
I remember the way you said my name.
I remember you.

I remember your embrace.
I remember your lap.
I remember the love we shared.
I remember you

I remember your soft grace.
I remember your stern voice.
I remember the memories we made.
I remember you.

I remember all the times.
I remember all the lines.

I remember every detail.
I remember you.

I will always Remember You.

For a Friend

When the day ends in red,
and rest doesn't come from bed.
When your mind stays busy,
and nothing is easy.

That's when you can count on me.

When you can't breathe slow,
and there's nothing new to know.
when anxiety claws at your brain,
and the sky is endless rain.

That's when you can count on me.

When your chest is weighty,
and your body feels eighty.
when your mind isn't calm,
and every emotion is a bomb.

That's when you can count on me.

You don't have to feel yourself,
or know what's happening next.
Just count on me.

I'll do my best.

You don't have to try so hard,
or save the day again.
Just count on me.
I'll stop the train.

Keep me in mind.
I'll be in your heart.
Right where I was from the start.

When the day ends in darkness,
and you can't contemplate the starkness.
When you feel useless,
and the tools you're used to are broken.

That's when you can count on me...

I'll be the sun.
I'll be the rain.
I'll be the darkness.
I'll be the pain.

I'll do my best to fill the empty space.
The place in your heart,
the place in your mind,
the place you don't like others to find.

I'll love you happy,

and I'll love you mad.
I'll love you funny,
and when you're sad.

All the days.
In all the ways.
That's when you can count on me.

Relationship Advice

I am me and you are you.
Together we are us.
We give, and we take.
We change, and we create.

Being us makes you better.
Being us makes me worse.

Our worlds collide and feelings divide.

Envy turns to obsession.
Greed creates a deep depression.

Helping you changes me.
Were we really meant to be?
Emotions erupt.
Actions corrupt.

Being us is getting hard.
We don't even know who WE are.

I've lost me.
You've lost you.
We've lost friends and created rifts.
Bridges we've burned and mistakes we've made.

Will we ever be okay?

I can't take it.
We won't make it.
I want me back.
I want my normal.
Back before we were ever formal.

So now I have to let you go.
We can't be us.
I'll just be me.
We'll just have to disagree.

So now I'll say goodbye forever.
I'll take me back,
You'll soon recover.
With time we'll both discover.

I'll still be me,
You'll still be you

Daddy

There's a special bond between a Daddy and a daughter.
Many a song has been written about a father's love.
Many a lyric has been composed about a daughter's rebellion.

The bond is special and the love is forever.

He's her first love.
She's his first real heartache.
The Hero and the Princess.
A love forged in blood and a bond moulded by the most innocent trust.

Daddy is the name of the first man she'll ever worship.
A daughter is a heartache and a dream to the man who helped create the vision.
Trying to tear the two apart is like trying to abstain from breathing.
Such a feat often ends in death.

The bond is special and the love is forever.

Sometimes the prince rides in.
Willing to woo the Princess for a moment of
bliss.
Unbeknownst to such a prince is the power of
the king.
For the Daddy will always hold a special kind of
grace over the heart of the Princess.

Daddy is and Daddy always will be.
Sometimes she fights it.
Sometimes he wars with her strength.
But they'll always come together.

The bond is special and the love is forever...

Between a Daddy and his Daughter.

The Other Man (For Dave)

To the other man.
I love you.
He's always going to resent your presence.
I find comfort in it.

Where he sees an intruder, I see part of my
peace.
He'll never understand our bond.
He won't get that we have the same interests.
He doesn't want to acknowledge there's merit to
your affection.

To the other man.
I love you.
He just doesn't understand.
I need you as much as I need him.

You're the rock that helped set the foundation.
The foundation that is me.
You gave me a wider range of Love.
You opened my heart.

To the other man.
I love you.
Honestly, I always have.
My life without you in it is sheltered and bereft.

I wouldn't understand the things I do,
or know the things I know,
If it weren't for your open heart,
and your open mind.

To the other man.
I love you.
You're the Companion I didn't know I needed.
You're the love that I was missing.

Hate is.

Hate is a strong emotion.
Stronger than love?

Hate eats away at the heart,
eats at the very soul of the being consumed.

Hate is a strong emotion.
Stronger than love?

Hate is raw and unnerving,
hate breeds past discontent,
hate flourishes and is consuming.

Hate is a strong emotion.
Stronger than love?

Hate is anger and resentment.
Hate is emotion in its most vulnerable state.

Hate is a strong emotion...

Love is.

Love is a strong emotion.
Stronger than hate?

Love is all consuming.
Love is powerful.
Love is more... always more.

Love is a strong emotion.
Stronger than hate?

Love is a new baby.
Love is a fresh relationship.
Love is joy.

Love is a strong emotion.
Stronger than hate?

Love is bliss.
Love is ignorance of the flaws of others.
Love is calm.

Love is a strong emotion.
Stronger than hate?

Love is....

Love is emotion in its most vulnerable state.

Love is the STRONGEST emotion...

Worse than death

People can do worse things than kill you.
People can betray you.
Betray your truth.

People can do worse things than kill you.
People can stop loving you.
Stop loving when you need them most.

People can do worse things than kill you.
People can leave.
Leave when you need their guidance most.

People can do worse things than kill you.
People can lose your trust.
Can say things you trusted them to keep secret.

People can do worse things than kill you.
Some people make themselves essential to you.
Then leave.

People can do worse things than kill you.

Cats

Have you ever wondered...
Why don't cats watch TV?
It is maybe, could it be, they would rather
scratch a flea?
Why don't cats watch TV?

Maybe they prefer the dreams they find in sleep,
while they're napping peacefully,
maybe that's why cats don't watch TV.

They like to play,
and they like to fight,
they like being silly,
so why don't cats watch TV?

Maybe they prefer soaking up the sun,
lazily stretching in the nice warm rays,
maybe that's why cats don't watch TV.

They like chasing bugs,
and the wandering laser light,
They like sneaking up on unsuspecting feet,
so why don't cats watch TV?

Have you ever wondered....

Why don't cats watch TV?
Is it maybe, could it be, they would rather
scratch a flea?
Why don't cats watch TV?

Lazy Days

Lazy days, feeling light.
napping,
talking,
reading,
music,
dancing.

Everyone needs a day,
where the worries of the world,
are aloud to melt away.

Forget the chores,
the dust can wait,
you need some time to play.

Forget the bills,
they'll be there tomorrow,
you need today to rest.

Forget the work,
the boss will understand,
if you take just one day for you.

Forget the deadlines,
tardiness can be forgiven,

your children need a hug...or seven.

Forget your plans,
cancel them,
your bed has claimed it's right to you.

Forget your an adult,
go back to Kindergarten,
if only just in your mind.

Let today be the day,
that you get to be yourself,
the silly child you left behind,
in the busy rush of life.

Remember who you were,
rest your weary brain,
life can restart later.

Have yourself the laziest day.
Nap,
Read,
Binge watch TV,
Crank up the tunes,
Dance,
Laugh.

Lazy days, feeling light...

Road Trip

If every there was a reason,
for a long road trip,
I would be a weary soul.

Road trips give you time to think,
ground yourself again,
escape the harsh reality.

If ever there was a reason,
for a long road trip,
I would be a heavy heart.

Road trips give you time to hurt,
reminisce about the time spent,
comes to terms with what's to come.

If ever there was a reason,
For a long road trip,
It would be a busy brain.

Road trips give you time to let go,
crank up the tunes,
roll down the windows,
let the breeze carry your worries away.

If ever there was a reason,
 for a long road trip,
it would be for no reason at all.

Sometimes you just need,
and open road,
a loud radio,
and a good friend,
to get back to yourself.

Falling

Falling leaves,
Feeling free,
From high atop the tree.

Rustle together,
Birds of a feather,
Chattering together.

The wind blows through,
The gracious view,
Laughter born anew.

Slipping,
Tripping,
Losing grip.

Loss of breath,
Burning chest,
Faithful friend laughs again.

Falling leaves,
Falling on me,
When I fell out the tree.

House Guest

There's a guest in the house.
A guest who's quite horrid.

They help themselves to the food,
They rearrange in every room.

They bring in animals,
And let their children wander free.

They don't seem to give a care about me.

I try to clean their mess,
Fix the cabinets they left awry,
I don't understand the reason why,

Because every time I turn around,
There's a new mess to be found.

I scream and shout,
I slam the doors,
It seems to make things even worse.

The leading lady had the gall,
To tell me I am the one who's wrong,

Disrespectful wench,
I wish someone could teach you some sense!

It appears to me they cannot even see,
All the dirty rotten things they do,
In the home they don't belong to.

Then tonight was the last straw!
They brought their own guest!

He was tall and dressed in black.
He wore the collar of a priest,
And he said to me, begone!

As if I am the one who doesn't belong?
It made me angry,
I was through!

I left that home,
Feeling blue,
My worst fear coming true.

Green

Trees and frogs and great big bogs.

Grass and leaves and crawling things.

Meadows, valleys, mountain sides.

Green is living.
Green smells free.
Green is soft and sweet.

Green is strong
Green is tall
Green is small

Green is inside us all
Green lives
Green breathes

Green is life

Dreaming

Falling softly into the abyss,
Deep and warm.

When suddenly I see,
Visions dancing aimlessly.

Sometimes happy,
Sometimes sad,
Sometimes scary,
Sometimes mad,

Some keep you on the edge,
Desperately waiting for the end,

Some consume you,
Fulfilling every desire you dare to have.

Some catch your breath,
Making your heart race.

Some are terrifying,
Awakening you screaming.

Some are silly,
They're nonsensical and fun.

Others leave you wishing,
You'll never wake up.